step-by-step
indonesian
cooking

Indonesian dishes are amongst the most
delicious in the world. Create your own with
these easy illustrated step-by-step instructions.

PERIPLUS

BASIC INDONESIAN PANTRY

Have the following ingredients on hand in your pantry to make it easier to prepare Indonesian-style dishes. Most ingredients can be found in your local supermarket or greengrocer. Some of the specialised ingredients can be found in Asian food stores. Or some like the fiery Sambal Oelek can be made at home.

Capsicum: Also known as red or green peppers.

Candlenuts (kemiri): From the candleberry tree, these nuts look like macadamia nuts and taste like brazil nuts. Available from Asian food stores.

Cardamom: Spice from the ginger family. Seeds are purchased whole, either in or out of their pods, or ground.

Chillies: Small red chillies are the hottest. The larger red chillies are milder and green chillies are milder still. Seeds are often discarded as they are the hottest part of the chilli.

Chinese Cabbage: Looks more like a lettuce or a huge head of celery than its name sake. It has a crisp and delicate flavour.

Coconut Cream: Thick white liquid that rises to the surface when coconut milk is left to stand.

Coconut Milk: This is not the juice from the inside of the fresh coconut but the liquid extracted from the white flesh.

Coriander: Indonesians use only the seed of the coriander plant, not the leaves or roots.

Cumin: An aromatic spice with a pungent flavour. Seeds are available whole or ground.

Curry Leaves: Are native to Southeast Asia and as its name suggests, lends a curry-like flavour to cooking.

Eggplant: Also known as aubergine.

Egg Noodles (fine, dry): Looks like fine spaghetti which has been wound into small bundles.

Ginger: Fresh ginger root is recommended, rather than dried. Indonesians also use laos and galangal which give a similar flavour and are occasionally available fresh from Asian food stores.

Lemon Grass: A herb with a citrus flavour. The bulb end imparts the most flavour. Usually added to a dish in large pieces and removed before serving, as lemon grass is very coarse. Fresh lemon grass is readily available from greengrocers

and Asian food stores. Dried lemon grass is also available but has a different flavour. To prepare lemon grass for adding to dish, either pound the stem to bruise the flesh and release the juices, or make cuts down the stem leaving one end intact.

Palm Sugar: Dark brown sugar made from the juice of the coconut palm flower. Sold in hard blocks; cut off required amount and crush it. Available from Asian food stores.

Peanut Oil: A light oil used extensively in Indonesian cooking. Coconut oil is also used.

Rice Flour : Is finely ground white or brown rice and often used as a thickener.

Sambal Oelek (or ulek): Hot chilli relish made of crushed chillies and salt. Other ingredients such as sugar and vinegar are sometimes added. See page 16 for recipe.

Sesame Oil : A strongly flavoured oil, used in small quantities.

Shrimp Paste (terasi): Extremely pungent, salty paste, sold in jars. Also available in hard blocks. Use sparingly.

Snow Peas: Bright green, delicate and sweet-flavoured pods of peas which are eaten whole.

Soy Sauce (kecap): Light soy sauce which is thin and salty. Kecap manis is dark soy sauce which is thick and sweet.

Spring Onions: Also known as shallots.

Tamarind (asam): From the tamarind tree. Can be bought as a firm block which must be simmered in water for a few minutes before squeezing out the liquid. Discard pulp and use liquid. Tamarind is also available as a paste or sauce which need no pre-preparation. It imparts a sour flavour to a dish.

Tofu (bean curd): A white gel made from soya beans.

Turmeric: A root spice similar to ginger, available mostly in its dried form. Adds a pungent flavour and gives a strong yellow colour.

Vermicelli: Are thin, white, slightly transparent rice noodles, wound into a skein shape.

3

Peel and devein prawns. Cut the white fish fillets into 2 cm cubes.

Pour enough hot water over the vermicelli to cover. Allow to stand.

SOUPS, SATAYS, ACCOMPANIMENTS

Indonesian dishes are renowned for their pungent sauces and seasoning pastes made by grinding fresh herbs with flavourings.

Seafood Laksa

A rice noodle dish.

Preparation time:
25 minutes
Cooking time:
10 minutes
Serves 4

500 g medium-sized
    green prawns
500 g white fish fillets
150 g vermicelli
1.5 L fish stock
4 spring onions,
    chopped
stem of lemon grass,
    10 cm long
1 tablespoon curry
    paste
1 teaspoon sambal
    oelek (see Basics)
1 teaspoon shrimp
    paste
1 teaspoon ground
    turmeric
1 cup coconut milk
1½ cups finely
    shredded lettuce
2 tablespoons chopped
    mint

1 Peel and devein prawns, cut fish fillets into 2 cm cubes.
2 Place vermicelli in large bowl. Pour over hot water to cover. Stand 10 minutes; drain.

3 Combine fish stock in a pan with spring onions, lemon grass, curry paste, sambal oelek, shrimp paste and turmeric, bring to the boil. Reduce heat to low, simmer for 3 minutes.
4 Add prawns, fish and coconut milk, simmer for 3 minutes. Remove lemon grass.
5 To serve, place lettuce and vermicelli into bowls, add soup, sprinkle with mint.

> ### HINT
> Water or chicken stock can be used instead of fish stock.

Add spring onions, lemon grass, pastes and turmeric to fish stock.

Add prawns, fish and coconut milk; simmer for 3 minutes.

Beef and Vegetable Soup

Preparation time:
10 minutes
Cooking time:
2½ hours
Serves 4

---

750 g piece beef
brisket on the bone
2 L water
2 bay leaves
stem of lemon grass,
10 cm long
1 tablespoon oil
1 onion, thinly sliced
from top to base
2 cloves garlic,
crushed
2 teaspoons grated
fresh ginger

10 candlenuts,
chopped roughly
(see Basics)
½ teaspoon ground
turmeric
1 tablespoon light soy
sauce
2 cups finely shredded
Chinese cabbage
1 cup bean sprouts
1 red capsicum,
thinly sliced

---

1 Place brisket in a large pan, fat side down. Fry over medium heat until brown.

2 Add water, bay leaves and lemon grass, bring to the boil. Reduce heat to low, cover, simmer for 2 hours. Remove brisket from stock, discard fat and bone, cut meat into 1 cm cubes, strain the stock. Return stock and meat to pan.

3 In a small pan, heat oil. Add onion, garlic, ginger, candlenuts and turmeric, stir-fry 3 minutes.

4 Place onion mixture in larger pan with meat and stock. Add soy sauce, simmer for 20 minutes.

5 Combine cabbage, bean sprouts and red capsicum in a large bowl. Pour enough hot water over to cover, leave to stand 2 minutes, drain.

6 To serve, place cabbage mixture in serving bowls, pour soup over the top.
Note: Soup can be prepared 3 days ahead up to step 3.

Add water, bay leaves and lemon grass to large pan, bring to the boil.

In a small pan, add candlenuts to onion, garlic, ginger, and turmeric.

Place onion mixture in larger pan with meat and stock.

Combine vegetables in large bowl, cover with hot water. Allow to stand.

Vegetable and Noodle Soup

Preparation time:
15 minutes
Cooking time:
10 minutes
Serves 4

---

100 g fine dried egg noodles	*1 large tomato, peeled and chopped*
1.5 L chicken stock	*1 tablespoon light soy sauce*
100 g cauliflower, cut in small florets	*1 teaspoon ground cumin*
100 g Chinese cabbage, cut in chunky pieces	*1 teaspoon ground coriander*
4 spring onions	

1 Soak noodles in hot water for a few minutes until strands are separated, drain.

2 Prepare vegetables, finely chop spring onions. Heat stock in a pan, add cauliflower, cabbage, chopped spring onions, tomato, soy sauce, cumin and coriander, bring to the boil, reduce heat, simmer uncovered for 5 minutes.

3 Add noodles, simmer further 3 minutes or until noodles are tender. Serve the soup immediately.

Prepare noodles, cauliflower, Chinese cabbage, spring onions and tomato.

Add chopped vegetables to pan with heated stock.

Add tomato, soy sauce, cumin and coriander; bring to the boil.

Add noodles, simmer further 3 minutes or until noodles are tender.

Chicken Satays with Peanut Sauce

Preparation time:
15 minutes
Cooking time:
10 minutes
Serves 8

---

8 chicken breast fillets
2 tablespoons light
   soy sauce
2 teaspoons lime juice
2 teaspoons sesame oil

PEANUT SAUCE
100 g roasted
   unsalted peanuts
3 spring onions,
   chopped

2 cloves garlic
1 teaspoon curry
   powder
1 teaspoon ground
   cumin
1/2 teaspoon ground
   coriander
1 tablespoon honey
2 teaspoons light soy
   sauce
1 cup water

---

1 Cut chicken fillets into long thin strips, thread onto 32 skewers in a weaving fashion.

2 To make Peanut Sauce: Combine peanuts in a food processor with spring onions, garlic, curry powder, cumin, coriander, honey, soy sauce and water, blend until smooth. Pour into a pan, stir over medium heat for 3 minutes or until sauce is reduced and thickened.

3 Cook chicken satays under preheated grill for 3 minutes on each side or until just cooked. During cooking, brush satays with combined soy sauce, lime juice and sesame oil. Serve immediately with hot Peanut Sauce.

Note: Peanut sauce may be made up a day in advance and stored in the refrigerator. Reheat over a low heat.

HINT
If using wooden skewers, soak them in water for at least 10 minutes before using to prevent the skewers burning during cooking.

Cut chicken fillets into long thin strips and thread onto skewers.

Combine Peanut Sauce ingredients in food processor, blend until smooth.

Heat Peanut Sauce over medium heat until reduced and thickened.

Brush chicken satays with combined soy sauce, lime juice and sesame oil.

Coconut Lamb Satay

Prepare a day ahead.

Preparation time:
10 minutes +
2 hours standing
Cooking time:
6 minutes
Serves 4

---

*4 lamb leg chops
(about 800 g)
1 small onion
1 clove garlic, crushed
1 tablespoon
tamarind sauce
1 tablespoon light soy
sauce*

*1 tablespoon vinegar
1 teaspoon sambal
oelek (see Basics)
¼ cup desiccated
coconut
2 tablespoons oil
1 teaspoon sesame oil*

---

1 Remove fat and bones from lamb chops and cut into 2 cm cubes.

2 Combine lamb with chopped onion, garlic, tamarind sauce, soy sauce, vinegar, sambal oelek and coconut. Marinate for 2 hours or refrigerate overnight.

3 Thread lamb onto skewers, brush with combined oils and cook under a hot preheated grill for 3 minutes.

HINT
Try this marinade with beef, chicken or pork.

Remove fat and bones from lamb chops and cut into 2 cm cubes.

Combine with onion, garlic, tamarind, soy, vinegar, sambal oelek and coconut. Mix.

Thread lamb cubes, marinated in sambal oelek mixture, onto skewers.

Brush skewered lamb with combined oils; cook on high about 3 minutes.

Peanut Sauce

Very popular.

250 g roasted unsalted peanuts
1 small onion, chopped
1 clove garlic, chopped
1 teaspoon chopped fresh ginger
1 teaspoon shrimp paste
1 teaspoon sambal oelek (see Basics)
1 tablespoon light soy sauce
1 tablespoon lemon juice
½ cup mango chutney
1 cup water

1 Chop peanuts and onions roughly. Combine all

Preparation time:
5 minutes
Cooking time:
5 minutes
Makes 2 cups

ingredients in a food processor, blend until smooth.

2 Pour mixture into a pan, bring to the boil. Reduce heat to low, simmer, stirring occasionally, for about 5 minutes, or until sauce has reduced and thickened.

Note: Use Peanut Sauce as an accompaniment to any meat or vegetable dish, a sauce for satays or a dipping sauce for vegetables (gado-gado).

Fried Bananas

Preparation time:
5 minutes
Cooking time:
3 minutes
Serves 4

A refreshing curry accompaniment.

3 large bananas
1 cup desiccated coconut
¼ cup peanut oil

1 Peel bananas, slice thickly on an angle, combine with coconut.

2 Heat oil in a frying pan, add banana, stir-fry over low heat until heated through and coconut begins to brown.

For Peanut Sauce: Chop the peanuts and prepare onion, garlic and ginger.

Combine all the ingredients in a food processor, blend until smooth.

For Fried Bananas: Add coconut to the sliced bananas.

Stir-fry bananas over a low heat until heated and coconut browned.

Sambal Oelek

Preparation time:
   10 minutes
Cooking time:
   15 minutes
Makes 1 cup

Use sambal oelek as a fiery accompaniment or add to recipes where chillies are required.

> *200 g small red chillies*
> *1 cup water*
> *1 teaspoon salt*
> *1 teaspoon sugar*
> *1 tablespoon vinegar*
> *1 tablespoon oil*

1   Remove stalks from chillies, chop chillies roughly. Combine in a pan with water, bring to the boil. Reduce heat to low, cover, simmer for 15 minutes.
2   Pour chillies into a food processor, add salt, sugar, vinegar and oil, blend until finely chopped. Store Sambal Oelek in a small glass jar (with a non metallic lid) in the refrigerator for up to two weeks.

HINT
Wear rubber or cotton gloves when handling chillies to avoid any contact with your skin. Kitchen scissors or knife can be used to cut the chillies. Carefully wash the knife and chopping board after preparation. The seeds are the hottest part of the chilli - they may be discarded, depending on your taste.

Cucumber Relish

Preparation time:
   10 minutes
Cooking time:
   Nil
Serves 4

> *1 large cucumber*
> *1 tablespoon palm sugar*
> *2 tablespoons vinegar*
> *1/2 teaspoon salt*
> *1 tablespoon chopped mint*

1   Peel cucumber, halve lengthways, scoop out seeds. Thinly slice cucumber, crossways.
2   Combine sugar, vinegar, salt and mint. Pour over cucumber. Serve as accompaniment.

For Sambal Oelek: Remove stalks from chillies, chop chillies roughly.

Add salt, sugar, vinegar, oil and chillies; blend until finely chopped.

For Cucumber Relish: Peel cucumber, halve lengthways, scoop out seeds.

Combine sugar, vinegar, salt and mint. Pour over the sliced cucumber.

Oil the pieces of calico and divide the rice between them.

Form rice into a log shape and roll up along the long side.

18

RICE & VEGETABLES

Rice is always the foundation of an Indonesian meal. It is customary to serve it with a curry and two or more vegetable dishes.

Steamed Rice Dumplings

> 2 cups long grain rice
> 2 cups water
> 4 pieces unbleached calico, 25 x 15 cm
> oil

Preparation time:
  5 minutes
Cooking time:
  2 hours 5 minutes
Serves 4

1 Rinse rice under cold running water, drain. Place in a pan with water, bring to the boil. Reduce heat to low, simmer uncovered for 5 minutes, or until water has been absorbed, and cool.

2 Oil the pieces of clean unbleached calico and divide rice between them. Form rice into a log shape along the long side, roll up to enclose the rice and tie ends with string.

3 Bring a large pan of water to the boil, add rice packages, cover and simmer over medium heat for 2 hours. Top up with water occasionally to keep packages afloat. Remove packages, refrigerate until cold and firm, unwrap before serving.

Note: Traditionally, rice dumplings are wrapped and cooked in blanched banana leaves. This method is recommended if leaves are available as they add flavour. Use toothpicks or string to tie the packages. Packaged banana leaves are often found in Asian specialty food stores.
Serve Rice Dumplings cold, sliced or cubed.

After rolling the calico to enclose the rice, tie the ends with string.

Slice firm dumplings into rounds, straight or diagonally. Serve cold.

Fragrant Coconut and Spice Rice

Preparation time:
5 minutes
Cooking time:
20 minutes
Serves 4

---

1 tablespoon oil
½ cup unsalted peanuts, shelled and roughly chopped
1 tablespoon desiccated coconut
1 cup coconut milk
2 cups water
stem of lemon grass, 10 cm long

8 curry leaves
2 spring onions, cut in 2 mm slices
1 teaspoon ground cumin
½ teaspoon ground cardamom
½ teaspoon ground turmeric
2½ cups long grain rice

---

1 Heat oil in pan. Add nuts, stir until golden; stir in coconut.

2 Add coconut milk and water to pan. Stir in lemon grass, curry leaves and spring onions, bring to the boil. Reduce heat, simmer, uncovered, for 2 minutes. Add cumin, cardamom and turmeric, bring to the boil. Add rice, cook, uncovered, until steam holes appear at the surface.

3 Cover pan with a tight fitting lid, reduce heat to very low, cook for 10 minutes. Lift lid, check if rice is cooked, continue cooking if required.

Note: Basmati or jasmine rice can be used instead of long grain rice, if preferred.

Avoid lifting the lid of the pan while rice is cooking, as all the steam will escape, resulting in gluggy rice.

HINT
The curry leaf is native to south east Asia and and as its name suggests lends a rich, curry-like flavour to Asian dishes.

Heat oil in pan. Add nuts, stir until lightly golden; stir in coconut.

Add coconut milk and water to golden nuts and coconut, mix well.

Stir in lemon grass, curry leaves and spring onions, bring to the boil.

Add cumin, cardamom and turmeric, bring to the boil. Add rice.

Nasi Goreng

A complete meal in a moment.

Preparation time:
15 minutes
Cooking time:
8 minutes
Serves 4 as a main course

500 g medium-sized green prawns	*1 teaspoon sambal oelek (see Basics)*
2 chicken thigh fillets	*1 tablespoon dark soy sauce*
2 eggs	*4 cups cooked rice*
3 tablespoons peanut oil	*4 spring onions, sliced on diagonal*
1 large carrot, cut into fine julienne strips	*spring onions and red capsicum, cut into strips and curled*
1 clove garlic, crushed	

1 Peel and devein prawns. Slice chicken fillets into thin strips.

2 Beat eggs with a fork until blended. Heat 1 tablespoon of oil in a frying pan, pour in eggs, cook over low heat until eggs have set, lift out. When omelette is cold, roll it up, slice thinly.

3 Heat remaining oil in frying pan, add prawns, chicken, carrot and garlic, stir-fry until browned.

4 Add sambal oelek, soy sauce, rice and spring onions, stir-fry until heated through. Serve garnished with omelette strips and spring onion and red capsicum curls, see Hint.

Note: Serve Nasi Goreng as a main meal on its own or as an accompaniment. You will need to cook 1½ cups of raw rice for this recipe. Cooked rice should be cooled before using for fried rice; this prevents glugginess.

HINT
To curl spring onion and capsicum, cut into fine strips and place in iced water, refrigerate.

Peel and devein prawns. Slice chicken fillets into strips and prepare vegetables.

Stir-fry prawns, chicken, carrot and garlic until hot and lightly browned.

Add sambal oelek, soy sauce, rice and
spring onions, stir-fry until heated.

Slice omelette and prepare spring onion
and red capsicum curls.

Nutty Corn Pancakes

Preparation time:
10 minutes
Cooking time:
10 minutes
Serves 4

---

2 corn cobs
1 cup roasted peanuts
3 spring onions, chopped
2 teaspoons grated fresh ginger
1 clove garlic, crushed
1 teaspoon ground cumin
1 egg, lightly beaten
2 tablespoons rice flour
1/2 cup peanut oil

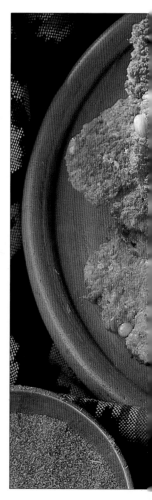

1 Remove niblets from cobs of corn with a sharp knife, combine in a food processor with peanuts, spring onions, ginger, garlic, and cumin, until finely chopped and slightly mushy. Transfer to bowl.

2 Add egg and rice flour, mix well.

3 Heat oil in pan, spoon tablespoons of mixture into pan and flatten with the back of the spoon. Cook over medium heat until golden brown on both sides. Drain on absorbent paper. **Note:** Serve these pancakes as a snack, entrée or with a main meal.

Process corn, peanuts, spring onions, ginger, garlic and cumin.

Add lightly beaten egg and rice flour to mixture and stir until combined.

Spoon tablespoons of the mixture into pan, flatten mixture with back of spoon.

Cook over a medium heat until pancakes are golden brown on both sides.

Curried Vegetables

Preparation time:
20 minutes
Cooking time:
20 minutes
Serves 4

---

2 medium potatoes, cut in 1 cm cubes
1 small eggplant, cut in 2 cm cubes
150 g snow peas, cut in 2 cm diagonals
200 g Chinese cabbage, shredded
1 carrot, cut in fine julienne strips
1 onion, cut into eight pieces
2 tablespoons peanut oil

2 cloves garlic, crushed
2 teaspoons grated fresh ginger
2 teaspoons curry powder
1 teaspoon grated lemon rind
1 tablespoon lemon juice
1/2 teaspoon shrimp paste
1 cup water
1 cup coconut milk

---

1 Peel and chop potatoes and eggplant into cubes. Prepare the snow peas, cabbage, carrot and onion.

2 Heat oil in frying pan, add onion, stir-fry 2 minutes. Add garlic, ginger and curry powder, stir-fry 2 minutes.

3 Add lemon rind, lemon juice, shrimp paste, water and coconut milk, bring to the boil.

4 Add potatoes and eggplant, simmer 15 minutes, stir occasionally. Add snow peas, cabbage and carrot, simmer for 5 minutes or until vegetables are tender.

Note: Any vegetables are suitable for this recipe. Choose a variety of coloured vegetables.

HINT
Chinese cabbage looks more like a lettuce or a huge head of a celery than its namesake. It has a crisp and delicate flavour.

Chop potatoes and eggplant. Prepare snow peas, cabbage, carrot and onion.

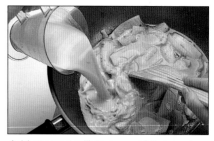
Add coconut milk to curry mixture and slowly bring mixture to the boil.

Add potatoes and eggplant; simmer uncovered 15 minutes; stir.

Add snow peas, cabbage and carrot; simmer until vegetables are tender.

Cold Vegetable Salad with Spice Dressing

Preparation time:
15 minutes
Cooking time:
8 minutes
Serves 4

---

10 spinach leaves, cut in 5 mm strips
300 g snake or ordinary beans, topped and tailed
80 g snow pea sprouts
100 g bean sprouts
1 red capsicum, cut in fine strips
1 Spanish onion, finely sliced from top to base

SPICE DRESSING
2 tablespoons peanut oil
1 clove garlic, crushed
1 teaspoon grated fresh ginger
1 small red chilli, chopped
2 tablespoons desiccated coconut
1 tablespoon brown vinegar
1/3 cup water

---

1   Remove stem from spinach, slice leaves thinly. Cut beans into 10 cm lengths. Remove long stems from snow pea sprouts.

2   Place beans in pan of boiling water, cook for 1 minute to blanch, drain. Combine spinach, beans, snow pea and bean sprouts, capsicum and onion in a bowl.

3   To make Dressing: Heat oil in a pan, add garlic, ginger, chilli and coconut, stir-fry over medium heat for 1 minute. Add vinegar and water, simmer for 1 minute, allow to cool.

4   To serve, add dressing to vegetables, toss until combined.

Note: Any blanched vegetables are suitable to use. Try to use a variety of vegetables for a colourful appearance.

HINT
Dressing can be added up to 30 minutes before serving.

Remove stems from each spinach leaf and slice the leaves thinly.

Combine spinach, beans, snow pea and bean sprouts, capsicum and onion.

For Spice Dressing, add vinegar and water to garlic, chilli and coconut.

Add dressing to vegetables and toss gently until well combined.

29

Pineapple Curry

A firm favourite.

Preparation time:
10 minutes
Cooking time:
15 minutes
Serves 4

1 medium pineapple	*2 spring onions, cut*
1 teaspoon cardamom	*in 2 cm pieces*
seeds	*2 teaspoons grated*
1 teaspoon coriander	*fresh ginger*
seeds	*4 candlenuts, roughly*
1 teaspoon cumin	*chopped*
seeds	*1 cup water*
1/2 teaspoon whole	*1 teaspoon sambal*
cloves	*oelek (see Basics)*
2 tablespoons oil	*1 tablespoon chopped*
	mint

1 Peel and halve pineapple, remove core, cut pineapple into 2 cm chunks.
2 Grind cardamom seeds, coriander seeds, cumin seeds and cloves in mortar and pestle.

3 Heat oil in a pan, add spring onions, ginger, candlenuts and spice mixture, stir-fry over low heat for 3 minutes.
4 Add water, sambal oelek, mint and pineapple, bring to

the boil. Reduce heat to low, simmer, covered, for 10 minutes, or until pineapple is tender but still holding its shape.
Note: If pineapple is a little tart, add 1-2 teaspoons of sugar.
A 450 g can of drained pineapple pieces can be used instead of fresh pineapple, if preferred or if fresh is unavailable.

HINT
This Pineapple Curry dish may be served as a vegetable accompaniment or simply add 500 g peeled and deveined, green prawns to make the dish a main course.

Peel and halve pineapple, remove core and cut pineapple into 2 cm chunks.

Grind cardamom, coriander and cumin seeds and cloves in mortar and pestle.

Add spring onions, ginger, candlenuts and spice mixture to pan.

Add water, sambal oelek, mint and pineapple, bring to the boil.

Deep Fried Spiced Tofu

Preparation time:
    10 minutes
Cooking time:
    10 minutes
Serves 4

375 g block firm tofu
½ cup rice flour
2 teaspoons ground coriander
1 teaspoon ground cardamom
1 clove garlic, crushed
½ cup water
oil, for deep frying

1 Drain tofu, cut into 1 cm thick slices.

2 Combine flour, coriander, cardamom and garlic in a bowl, add water, stir until smooth.

3 Heat oil in a pan. Dip tofu slices into spice mixture, coat thickly.

4 Lower slices into heated oil, three at a time, cook on medium heat for 1 minute on each side or until crisp and golden brown, drain on absorbent paper. Repeat with remaining slices.

Note: Tofu is available from specialty Asian stores and health food stores. Serve tofu with stir-fried vegetables and any sauce of your choice, e.g. peanut, chilli or soy sauce, the tofu soaks up the flavours.

Cut drained block of firm tofu into 1 cm thick slices.

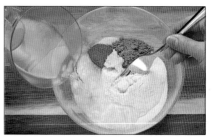

Add water to flour, coriander, cardamom and garlic, stir.

Dip tofu slices into spice mixture, coat them thickly and evenly.

Lower slices into heated oil, cook until crisp and lightly golden brown.

Slice beef thinly, flatten slices with a meat mallet, if necessary.

Combine garlic, lemon rind, ginger, coriander, turmeric, palm sugar and oil.

MEAT & POULTRY

Many of these dishes can be made up earlier than required to allow the flavours to develop, and heated up just before serving, if they are to be served hot.

Beef Fillet in Toasted Coconut

A party pleaser.

Preparation time:
15 minutes +
1 hour standing
Cooking time:
10 minutes
Serves 4

500 g piece beef eye fillet
2 cloves garlic, crushed
2 teaspoons grated lemon rind
1 teaspoon grated fresh ginger
2 teaspoons ground coriander
½ teaspoon ground turmeric
2 teaspoons palm sugar
3 tablespoons peanut oil
½ cup desiccated coconut
3 spring onions, cut into thin strips

1 Slice beef thinly, flatten slices with a meat mallet if necessary.

2 Combine garlic, lemon rind, ginger, coriander, turmeric, palm sugar and 2 tablespoons of the oil in a bowl. Add beef slices, toss well to coat. Leave to stand at least 1 hour.

3 Heat remaining tablespoon of oil in a frying pan, add beef, stir-fry until brown. Add coconut and spring onions, stir-fry for 1 minute, or until brown. Serve with steamed rice.

HINT
Beef fillet will slice more easily if placed into the freezer for about one hour before slicing.

Stir-fry marinated beef in pan, until meat is brown.

Add coconut and spring onions and stir-fry for 1 minute. Serve immediately.

35

Lamb Curry

A popular dish.

Preparation time:
15 minutes
Cooking time:
1 hour
Serves 6

1.5 kg leg of lamb, boned
1 tablespoon coriander seeds
2 teaspoons black peppercorns
2 teaspoons cardamom seeds
2 teaspoons cumin seeds
6 whole cloves
1/2 cinnamon stick, crumbled

2 tablespoons oil
1 large onion, chopped
2 cloves garlic, crushed
2 teaspoons grated fresh ginger
stem of lemon grass, 10 cm long
400 g can tomatoes
2 cups water
1 cup coconut milk

---

1   Remove fat from lamb, cut lamb into 2.5 cm cubes.
2   Finely grind coriander seeds, peppercorns, cardamom seeds, cumin seeds, cloves and cinnamon.
3   Heat oil in a pan, add lamb in three batches, fry until brown, remove.
4   Add onion, garlic, ginger and lemon grass to pan, stir-fry until onion is tender. Add spice mixture, stir-fry for 3 minutes.
5   Return lamb to pan with undrained, crushed tomatoes, water and coconut milk, bring to the boil. Reduce heat to low, simmer, uncovered, stirring often, for 1½ hours, or until lamb is tender.
Note: This curry is very mild. If you prefer a spicier one, add 1 to 4 chopped red chillies.

HINT
Most Indonesians are Muslims and therefore do not eat pork. Instead they eat lamb, beef and goat.

Cut lamb. Grind coriander, peppercorns, cardamom, cumin, cloves and cinnamon.

Heat oil in pan, add lamb and fry until brown then remove.

Add onion, garlic, ginger and lemon grass to pan, stir-fry.

Add undrained tomatoes, water and coconut milk to lamb.

Spicy Meatballs with Tomato Vermicelli

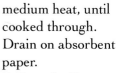

Preparation time:
15 minutes
Cooking time:
15 minutes
Serves 4

---

500 g minced beef
1 cup mashed potato
2 teaspoons sambal oelek (see Basics)
1 tablespoon light soy sauce
1 tablespoon ground coriander
1 teaspoon ground cumin
1 teaspoon ground cardamom
½ teaspoon ground nutmeg

1 egg, lightly beaten
¾ cup peanut oil

TOMATO VERMICELLI
425 g can tomatoes, crushed
1 cup water
1 onion, chopped
2 cloves garlic, crushed
1 tablespoon light soy sauce
100 g vermicelli

---

1 Combine beef in a bowl with potato, sambal oelek, soy sauce, coriander, cumin, cardamom, nutmeg and egg. Shape tablespoons of mixture into balls.

2 Heat oil in a frying pan, add meatballs in a single layer, fry on all sides, over medium heat, until cooked through. Drain on absorbent paper.

3 To make Tomato Vermicelli: Combine undrained, crushed tomatoes, water, onion, garlic and soy sauce in a pan, bring to the boil, reduce heat to low, simmer, uncovered, for 10 minutes. Add vermicelli, simmer for 3 minutes, or until vermicelli is soft. Serve with meatballs.

Note: Vermicelli noodles are available in supermarkets and specialty Asian stores.

> **HINT**
> Instant mashed potato can be used for this recipe.

Shape tablespoons of beef, spice and egg mixture into balls.

Heat oil in pan; add meatballs and fry over medium heat on all sides.

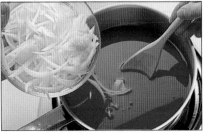

Add onion and garlic to crushed tomatoes and water.

Add vermicelli to tomato mixture and simmer until vermicelli are soft.

Beef Rendang

Serve with rice.

Preparation time:
15 minutes
Cooking time:
2 hours
Serves 4

---

1 kg rump steak
2 onions, chopped
4 cloves garlic,
    chopped
1 tablespoon chopped
    fresh ginger
4 small red chillies,
    chopped
½ cup water

2 teaspoons ground
    coriander
2 tablespoons
    tamarind sauce
1 teaspoon ground
    turmeric
10 curry leaves
stem of lemon grass,
    10 cm long
4 cups coconut milk

---

1 Remove fat and sinew from steak, cut meat into 3 cm cubes, place in a bowl.

2 In food processor, combine onions, garlic, ginger, chillies and water, blend until smooth. Add the mixture to steak.

3 Add coriander, tamarind sauce, turmeric, curry leaves and lemon grass, stir until combined. Transfer to pan; stir in coconut milk. Bring to the boil, reduce heat to medium, simmer, uncovered, for 1 hour, stirring occasionally. Reduce heat to very low, simmer 30 minutes, stirring frequently, until the meat is very tender and liquid has been absorbed. Remove lemon grass before serving.

Note: It is necessary to stir the Beef Rendang often during the last 30 minutes of cooking to prevent coconut milk from separating and to avoid sticking. This distinctive and delicious curry is cooked very slowly for a long time, until the meat is very succulent and all the coconut milk has been absorbed.

Prepare onions, garlic, fresh ginger and small red chillies.

Add blended onions, spices, chillies and water to the cubed steak.

Add coriander, tamarind sauce, turmeric, curry leaves and lemon grass; stir.

Stir in coconut milk. Bring to the boil, reduce heat and simmer.

Baked Lemon Spatchcocks

A tangy main dish.

4 spatchcocks
  (500 g each)
2 onions, chopped
2 red chillies
2 cloves garlic,
  crushed
1 spring onion,
  chopped
¼ cup peanut oil
¼ cup lemon juice

Preparation time:
  15 minutes +
  1 hour standing
Cooking time:
  40 minutes
Serves 4

1 Cut spatchcocks in half along the breast and backbone. Press down on each half to flatten slightly.

2 Combine onion, chopped chilli, garlic, oil and lemon juice in food processor, blend until smooth, spoon over spatchcocks.

Allow to stand 1 hour, or overnight.

3 Using tongs, remove spatchcocks from marinade, place in a baking dish in single layer. Bake at 180°C for 40 minutes, or until cooked and browned. Brush occasionally with marinade.

HINTS

This marinade is suitable for any chicken pieces, for example thighs and breasts.

Cut spatchcocks in half along the breast and back bone.

Combine onion, chilli, garlic, oil and lemon juice; blend until smooth.

Spread marinade over the spatchcocks. Allow to stand at least 1 hour.

Place spatchcocks in a single layer in a baking dish.

Tamarind Chicken

Use mild chillies.

Preparation time:
15 minutes +
2 hours standing
Cooking time:
30 minutes
Serves 4

---

4 chicken thighs
4 chicken drumsticks
1/3 cup tamarind sauce
2 teaspoons ground
coriander
1 teaspoon ground
turmeric
2 cloves garlic, crushed

2 tablespoons peanut
oil
2 red chillies, finely
chopped
6 spring onions,
finely chopped
oil, for deep frying

---

1 Remove skin from chicken pieces, place chicken in a pan of water. Simmer, covered, for 15 minutes, or until cooked through, drain, cool.

2 Combine tamarind sauce, coriander, turmeric and garlic, add to chicken, toss well to coat. Leave to stand at least 2 hours, preferably overnight.

3 Heat peanut oil in a frying pan, add chillies and spring onions, stir-fry over low heat for 3 minutes, set aside.

4 Heat oil for deep frying in a large pan Cook chicken in three batches on medium heat for 5 minutes, or until chicken is hot and golden brown. Lift out, drain on absorbent paper, keep warm while frying remaining chicken.

5 Serve the chicken pieces with a spoonful of the chilli mixture on the side.

Note: To tone down the fire still further, choose green chillies instead.

> HINT
> Marinated chicken pieces can be grilled instead of deep fried, if preferred.

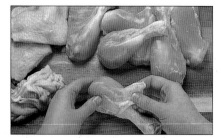

Remove skin from chicken pieces, place chicken in a pan of water.

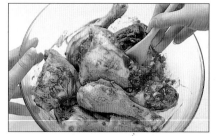

Toss chicken through combined spice mixture. Coat the chicken well.

Heat oil, add chillies and spring onions, stir-fry over low heat.

Deep-fry chicken until golden brown. Lift out, drain on absorbent paper.

Pineapple Chicken Drumsticks

Preparation time:
20 minutes
Cooking time:
35 minutes
Serves 4

---

8 chicken drumsticks
1 small pineapple
2 tablespoons peanut
* oil*
1 onion, chopped
1 teaspoon grated
* fresh ginger*

1 clove garlic, crushed
2 small red chillies, cut
* into thin rounds*
1/3 cup coconut milk
1/2 cup water

---

1 Using a large, sharp knife, cut off the bone end of the drumsticks. Remove and discard skin and fat from the drumsticks.

2 Peel and core pineapple, cut into 2 cm cubes.

3 Heat oil in frying pan, add chicken pieces and onion, fry on all sides until brown. Add pineapple, toss for 1 minute. Add fresh ginger, garlic and red chilli, fry 1 minute.

4 Pour in coconut milk and water, bring to the boil, reduce heat to low, cover, simmer, stirring occasionally, for 30 minutes, or until the chicken is tender.

Remove skin and fat from the chicken. Stir-fry chicken pieces and onion in pan.

Add pineapple to chicken and onion - toss for 1 minute.

Add ginger, garlic and chilli to chicken mixture, fry 1 minute.

Pour in coconut milk and water, bring to the boil, reduce heat to low.

Pandang Chicken

A light, aromatic dish with a tangy flavour.

Preparation time:
15 minutes +
1 hour standing
Cooking time:
40 minutes
Serves 4

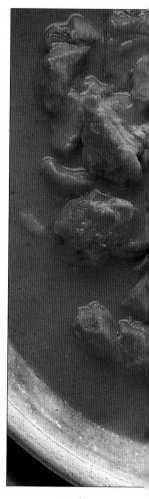

---

1 kg chicken thigh fillets, cut into 3cm cubes
½ cup lime juice
250 g ripe tomatoes
1 cup water
3 small red chillies, seeded and sliced in short, thin strips

2 teaspoons grated fresh ginger
2 cloves garlic, crushed
1 teaspoon ground turmeric
stem of lemon grass, 10 cm long
1 cup coconut cream

---

1 Combine chicken with lime juice; stand for about 1 hour.

2 Chop tomatoes combine with water, blend until smooth; strain into a pan.

3 Add chillies, ginger, garlic, turmeric, lemon grass (remove before serving) and undrained chicken. Bring to boil, reduce heat, cover, simmer for 30 minutes.

4 Add coconut cream, simmer, uncovered, for 10 minutes.

Chop the chicken thigh fillets into 3 cm cubes. Combine with lime juice.

Process chopped tomato and water until smooth. Strain into a pan.

Add chillies, ginger, garlic, turmeric, lemon grass and undrained chicken.

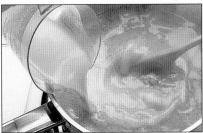

Stir in coconut cream, simmer uncovered, for 10 minutes.

49

Combine coconut cream, rind, juice, soy sauce and shrimp paste in a bowl.

Heat oil in pan. Stir-fry onions and prawns until tender.

SEAFOOD

Islands of Indonesia abound in seafood. The dishes are spicy and often creamy with the liberal use of coconut cream.

Prawns in Spices and Coconut Cream

Preparation time:
15 minutes
Cooking time:
5 minutes
Serves 4

1.25 kg green king prawns
200 mL coconut cream
1 teaspoon grated lime or lemon rind
1 tablespoon lime or lemon juice
2 teaspoons light soy sauce
½ teaspoon shrimp paste
1 tablespoon peanut oil
1 small onion, cut into 8 pieces
spring onions and red capsicum, cut into strips and curled, to serve

1 Peel prawns leaving tail intact, remove back vein.
2 Combine coconut cream, rind, juice, soy sauce and shrimp paste in a bowl.
3 Heat oil in a frying pan, add onion, stir-fry until tender.

Add prawns, stir-fry for 2 minutes.
4 Add coconut cream mixture, stir over heat for 3 minutes or until sauce has reduced and thickened. Serve garnished with spring onion and red capsicum curls.

HINTS
This dish can be cooked ahead of time. Reheat just before serving.
To make spring onion and/or red pepper curls, cut into very fine 6 cm long strips. Place in bowl of iced water, refrigerate until curled. Drain before using.

Add coconut cream mixture and stir over heat for 3 minutes.

Slice spring onion ends, red capsicum; place into iced water, for garnish.

King Prawns with Peanuts

Preparation time:
1 hour 20 minutes
Cooking time:
3 minutes
Serves 4

1.25 kg green king
prawns
4 spring onions,
chopped
1 clove garlic, crushed
1 teaspoon grated
fresh ginger
1 teaspoon sambal
oelek (see Basics)
1 teaspoon ground
coriander

1/2 teaspoon ground
turmeric
1 teaspoon grated
lemon rind
1 tablespoon lemon
juice
2/3 cup chopped
roasted, unsalted
peanuts
2 tablespoons peanut
oil

1 Peel prawns leaving tail intact, remove back vein.
2 Combine prawns with spring onions, garlic, ginger, sambal oelek, coriander, turmeric, lemon rind and juice and peanuts. Leave to stand for at least 1 hour.
3 Heat oil in frying pan, add prawn mixture, stir-fry over high heat for about 3 minutes or until prawns are cooked.

Peel green king prawns leaving tail intact, remove back vein.

Mix prawns, spring onions, garlic, ginger, sambal oelek, coriander and turmeric.

Add lemon rind and juice and peanuts. Allow to stand.

Add prawn mixture to heated oil, and stri-fry until prawns are cooked.

Baked Fish with Spices

Preparation time:
  15 minutes
Cooking time:
  30 minutes
Serves 2

---

2 x 300 g whole white
  fish
1 onion, chopped
1 clove garlic, crushed
1 teaspoon chopped
  fresh ginger
1 teaspoon chopped
  lemon rind

2 tablespoons
  tamarind sauce
1 tablespoon light soy
  sauce
1 tablespoon peanut
  oil

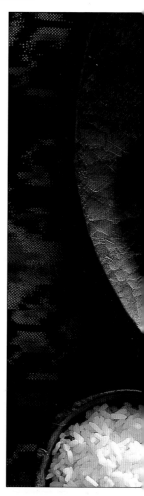

1 Place fish onto large pieces of foil. Make three deep incisions with sharp knife on each side of fish.

2 In a food processor, combine onion, garlic, ginger, lemon rind, tamarind sauce, light soy sauce and peanut oil, blend until the mixture is smooth.

3 Spread mixture on both sides and inside the fish.

4 Wrap foil around fish, secure firmly. Place fish in a baking dish, bake at 180°C for 30 minutes, or until fish is just cooked.

Place fish onto large pieces of foil. Score sides of the fish with a sharp knife.

Process onion, garlic, ginger, lemon rind, tamarind sauce, soy sauce and oil.

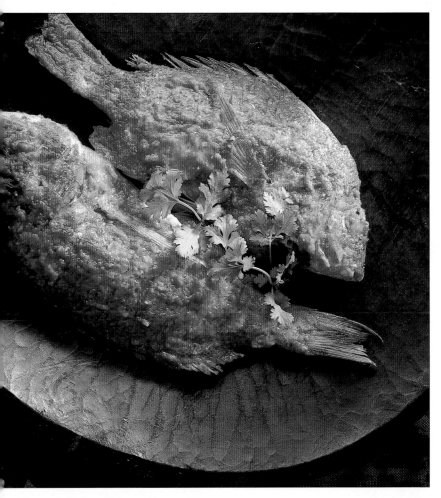

Spread onion and garlic mixture on both sides and inside the fish.

Wrap foil around the fish and secure firmly. Place in baking dish and bake.

Fish Cutlets with Curry Sauce

Preparation time:
10 minutes
Cooking time:
15 minutes
Serves 4

---

1 tablespoon oil	*2 teaspoons light soy*
1 onion, sliced thickly	*sauce*
from top to base	*2 teaspoons lemon*
1 teaspoon grated	*juice*
fresh ginger	*1 cup water*
8 candlenuts, chopped	*4 fish cutlets, from*
into 8 pieces	*tail end*
1 teaspoon curry	*2 spring onions,*
powder	*chopped*

1 Heat oil in frying pan, add onion, stir-fry until tender. Add ginger, candlenuts and curry powder, stir-fry over low heat for 3 minutes.

2 Add soy sauce, lemon juice and water, bring to the boil. Reduce heat and simmer for 3 minutes.

3 Add fish cutlets in single layer. Cover, simmer 5 minutes on each side or until just cooked through. Sprinkle with chopped spring onions.

Add ginger, candlenuts and curry powder to stir-fried onion.

Add soy sauce, lemon juice and water to onion and curry mixture, bring to the boil.

Place fish cutlets in single layer over onion mixture, cover and simmer.

Sprinkle chopped spring onions over the fish cutlets and onion mixture.

Add egg and milk mixture to sifted plain and rice flours, coconut and sugar.

Pour 2 tablespoons of mixture into heated pan, cook until golden and turn.

DESSERTS

Indonesians make good use of fresh tropical fruits and delicately flavour them with coconut cream and palm sugar for their desserts.

Mango Crepes with Coconut Sauce

Preparation time:
10 minutes
Cooking time:
15 minutes
Serves 4

½ cup plain flour
½ cup brown rice flour
½ cup desiccated coconut
2 tablespoons caster sugar
2 eggs, lightly beaten
1¼ cups milk
2 mangoes, peeled and chopped
1 cup coconut cream
1 tablespoon palm sugar

Combine sifted plain and rice flours in a bowl with coconut and sugar. Add combined eggs and milk, whisk until smooth.

Grease an 18 cm frying pan, heat to medium. Pour in 2 tablespoons of mixture, cook until lightly browned underneath. Turn crêpe, cook for 1 minute, remove. Repeat with remaining mixture.

3 Divide mango between crepes, roll up, tucking in ends.

4 Combine coconut cream and palm sugar in a pan, stir over heat until sugar has dissolved. Pour over crêpes to serve.

Note: If fresh mangoes are unavailable, use canned mangoes, or use any fresh fruit.

HINT
Palm sugar is a dark brown sugar made from the juice of the coconut palm flower.

Spoon mango filling onto crêpes and roll up, taking care to tuck in the ends.

Combine coconut cream and palm sugar in a pan and stir until sugar dissolves.

Hot Bananas with Cinnamon Coconut Sauce

Preparation time:
5 minutes
Cooking time:
10 minutes
Serves 4

4 large bananas	*2 tablespoons sugar*
	½ teaspoon ground
CINNAMON	*cinnamon*
COCONUT SAUCE	*1⅓ cups coconut milk*
1 tablespoon plain flour	

1 Remove ends from bananas, place bananas into a covered steamer over a pan of boiling water, cook for 5 minutes.

2 Use tongs and a knife to peel off banana skins.

3 To make Cinnamon Coconut Sauce: Add flour, sugar and cinnamon to a pan and stir until well combined. Add coconut milk and blend until smooth. Stir constantly over medium heat until mixture boils and thickens. Simmer for 2 minutes. Serve Cinnamon Coconut Sauce with hot bananas.

Note: Banana skins will turn black during cooking but the bananas will be golden inside.

Rinse bananas and remove ends from each one using a sharp knife.

Place bananas into a covered steamer over a pan of boiling water and cook.

Carefully peel off skin using tongs and a knife. Bananas should be golden inside.

Combine flour, sugar, cinnamon and coconut milk. Simmer to thicken.

Chocolate Spice Cake

Preparation time:
30 minutes
Cooking time:
45 minutes
Makes 1 x 20 cm cake

185 g butter	*¾ cup milk*
1 cup caster sugar	*100 g dark chocolate,*
4 eggs	*grated*
1½ cups plain flour	*2 teaspoons ground*
1 cup self-raising	*mixed spice*
flour	*icing sugar*

1 Preheat oven to 180°C. Cream butter and sugar with an electric mixer until light and creamy. Add eggs one at a time, beat until combined between additions.

2 Fold in sifted plain and self-raising flours with milk.

3 Divide mixture into two portions. Fold chocolate into one portion and mixed spice into the other.

4 Spoon chocolate mixture into a greased 20 cm baba pan. Spoon spice mixture over the top. Smooth with spoon.

5 Bake for 45 minutes, or until cake is cooked through. Turn onto wire rack to cool. Serve dusted with icing sugar.

Fold in sifted flours and milk to creamed butter and sugar and egg mixture.

Combine mixed spice with half mixture, fold chocolate into remaining half.

Spoon chocolate mixture over base of prepared pan and smooth over.

Spoon spice mixture over the top of the chocolate and smooth over with spoon.

INDEX